HOW WOULD YOU SURVIVE AS AN
AZTEC?

Written by
Fiona Macdonald

Illustrated by
Mark Bergin

Created & Designed by
David Salariya

FRANKLIN WATTS
A Division of Grolier Publishing
NEW YORK • LONDON • HONG KONG • SYDNEY
DANBURY, CONNECTICUT

David Salariya   *Director*
Penny Clarke   *Editor*
Dr. Nicholas James   *Consultant*

FIONA MACDONALD

studied history at Cambridge University and at the University of East Anglia, where she is a part-time tutor in medieval history. She has also taught in schools and adult education, and is the author of numerous books for children on historical topics, including **Cities** in the *Timelines* series.

MARK BERGIN

studied illustration at Eastbourne College of Art. Since leaving art school in 1983, he has specialized in historical reconstructions and architectural cross sections. He has illustrated four titles in the award-winning *Inside Story* series and is a major contributor to the *Timelines* and *X-Ray Picture Book* series. Mark Bergin lives in England with his wife and daughter.

DAVID SALARIYA

was born in Dundee, Scotland, where he studied illustration and printmaking. He has illustrated a wide range of books on botanical, historical, and mythical subjects. He has created and designed many new series of books for publishers worldwide. In 1989 he established The Salariya Book Company. He lives in England with his wife, the illustrator Shirley Willis.

©THE SALARIYA BOOK CO LTD MCMXCIV

Library of Congress Cataloging-in-Publication Data

Macdonald, Fiona.
    How would you survive as an Aztec? / written by Fiona Macdonald;
    illustrated by Mark Bergin; created & designed by David Salariya.
    p. cm. - (How would you survive?)
    Includes index.
    ISBN 0-531-14348-1 (lib. bdg.)   0-531-15304-5 (pbk.)
    1. Aztecs – Juvenile literature. [1.Aztecs, Medieval. 2. Middle Ages.]
    I. Bergin, Mark, ill. II. Title III. Series.
FI218.75.M835 1995
972'.01N – dc20   54-28068
                                    CIP AC

First American Edition 1995 by FRANKLIN WATTS
A Division of Grolier Publishing
Sherman Turnpike
Danbury, CT 06816
First Paperback Edtion 1997

DR. NICHOLAS JAMES

studied at the universities of Oxford, London, and Michigan. His research specialization is Mexico, where he has worked. He teaches Native American history at Birkbeck College, University of London.

CONTENTS

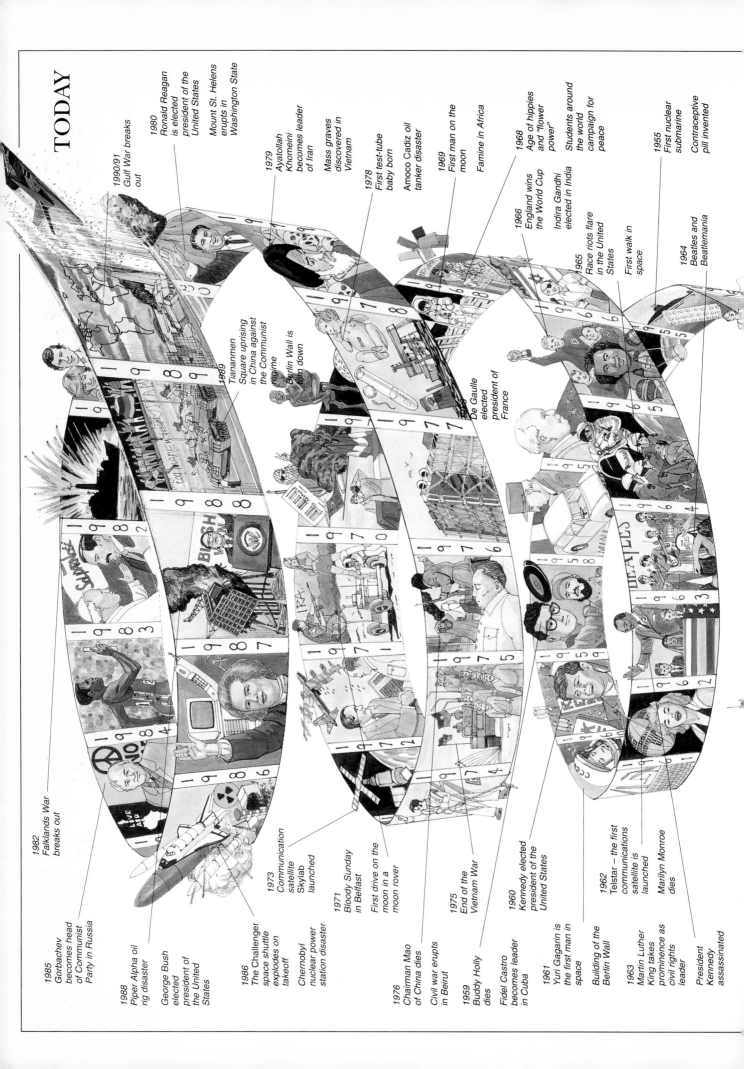

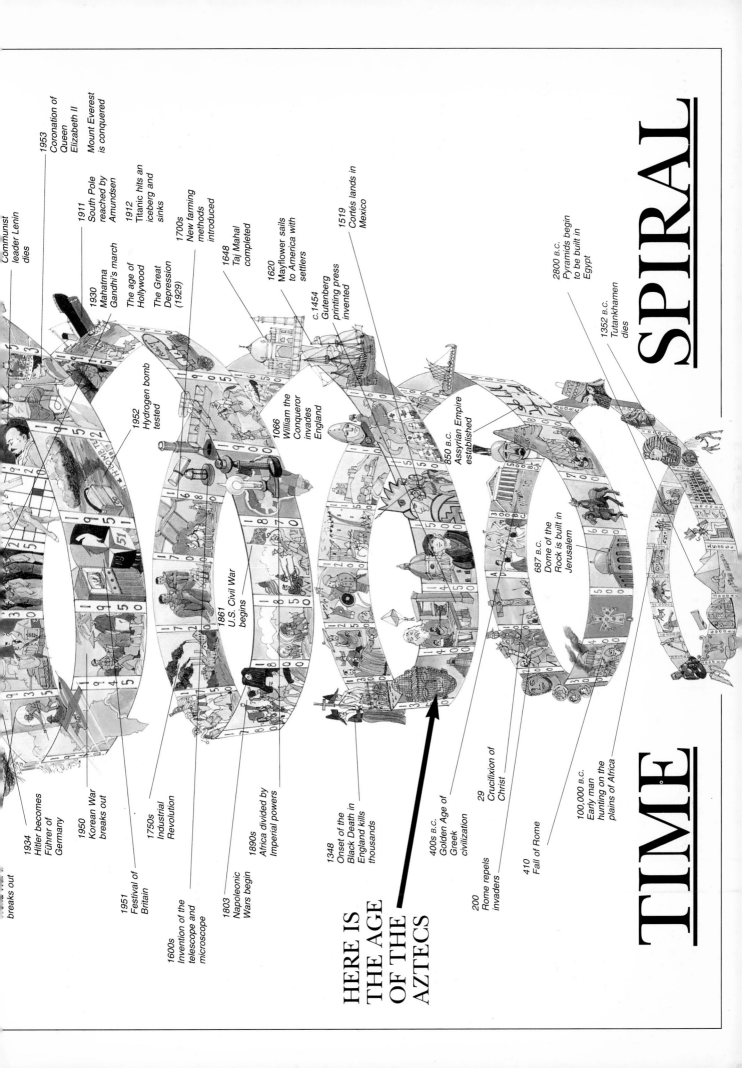

SPIRAL

TIME

HERE IS THE AGE OF THE AZTECS

Communist leader Lenin dies

1953 Coronation of Queen Elizabeth II

Mount Everest is conquered

1911 South Pole reached by Amundsen

1912 Titanic hits an iceberg and sinks

1700s New farming methods introduced

1930 Mahatma Gandhi's march

The age of Hollywood

The Great Depression (1929)

1648 Taj Mahal completed

1620 Mayflower sails to America with settlers

c.1454 Gutenberg printing press invented

1519 Cortés lands in Mexico

2800 B.C. Pyramids begin to be built in Egypt

1352 B.C. Tutankhamen dies

1952 Hydrogen bomb tested

1066 William the Conqueror invades England

850 B.C. Assyrian Empire established

687 B.C. Dome of the Rock is built in Jerusalem

breaks out

1934 Hitler becomes Führer of Germany

1950 Korean War breaks out

1951 Festival of Britain

1600s Invention of the telescope and microscope

1750s Industrial Revolution

1803 Napoleonic Wars begin

1890s Africa divided by Imperial powers

1861 U.S. Civil War begins

1348 Onset of the Black Death in England kills thousands

400s B.C. Golden Age of Greek civilization

29 Crucifixion of Christ

200 Rome repels invaders

410 Fall of Rome

100,000 B.C. Early man hunting on the plains of Africa

Land of Contrasts

YOU HAVE TRAVELED back in time to the Aztec period, around A.D. 1300–1500. What do you see? You will see that you are visiting a land of extremes: high mountains, dry deserts, and shallow, swampy lakes. This is the Aztecs' homeland, in the great central valley of modern Mexico. It is a land of great contrasts. There are snowy peaks, tropical rainforests, sandy beaches, smoking volcanoes, and bleak, windswept steppes.

A Harsh Climate

UP IN THE MOUNTAINS, the sun beats down pitilessly during the daytime, with temperatures reaching over 80°F (27°C) in the summer months. But on winter nights it becomes bitterly cold, with strong winds, sudden frosts, hail and snow. Down in the valleys it is milder, because there is a moist, cloudy haze. Wherever you live, you wait anxiously for the winter rains to begin. If there is a drought, crops will not grow and many people will die.

Wildlife & Plants

OVER MILLIONS OF YEARS, plants and animals have evolved to survive in the conditions found in Aztec lands. In the deserts, you will see many varieties of cactus, along with spiders, snakes, and lizards. In the lakes, there are fish, frogs, and turtles. Cocoa and vanilla grow in the tropical lands nearby; hummingbirds and jaguars live in the rain forests. If you are lucky, you might see armadillos, opossums, and deer, as well.

City & State

AZTECS RULE a mighty state (see pages 8–9), centered on the city of Tenochtitlan. Aztec legends say they came from the north, probably in 1345, guided by their gods. But evidence for this is lacking. The Aztec emperor – the Tlatoani ("Speaker") – lives at the heart of the city, in a magnificent palace. He rules with the help of the army, the nobles, and many officials. He has a male assistant, called Cihuacoatl (Snake Woman).

Tribute & Trade

COMPARED WITH OTHER NATIONS, the Aztecs are rich. Their wealth comes from tribute – taxes paid in goods by conquered peoples – and from trade. But, as you walk through the city streets, or along footpaths beside the fields, most ordinary men and women look poor. Why? Because the tribute is paid mainly to the Tlatoani, the nobles, and the army commanders. And the rich merchants take most of the profits from trade.

Hunting

READY? IT'S TIME to go hunting. What you catch will depend on where you go; there are hares and rabbits on the mountains, and wild turkeys and boar in the valleys. Or what about hunting jaguars in the forests, to get their beautiful spotted skins? You could use blowpipes to kill forest birds for their valuable feathers. Or perhaps you'd rather go to the lake? There are plenty of ducks and geese there for you to catch.

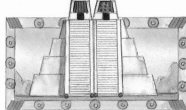

Gods & Spirits

GODS AND GODDESSES rule the Aztec world. Aztecs say that their crops ripen and their armies win battles because the gods help them. If the gods become angry, they might stop helping. So it is important to keep them happy with prayers and sacrifices. Aztecs have two kinds of god: ancient gods like Tlaloc, the rainmaker, worshiped in the region for thousands of years, and their own gods, like Huitzilopochtli, the war god.

Temples & Priests

THE BIGGEST BUILDINGS in any Aztec town are the temples, built on top of huge pyramids, where the gods and goddesses are worshiped. The Aztec capital, Tenochtitlan, had several temples in a sacred precinct, or square. Temples are staffed by priests and priestesses; many are skilled astronomers and scribes. Other duties include supervising sacrifices and "feeding" statues of the gods with human hearts.

Death & Danger

HOW OLD ARE YOU? If you are more than five years old, then, by Aztec standards, you are lucky to be alive. Probably at least half the babies born to Aztec families die before that age. Adults face death and danger, too. Women die in childbirth; men are killed in battle or chosen as a sacrifice to the gods. Criminals might be executed if they break the law more than once. And everyone is at risk from hunger and disease.

Food & Farming

WHEN THE AZTECS ARRIVED in Mexico from the north, they settled on a rocky island. Aztec legends say that, at first, the Aztecs lived on snakes and cactus. But Aztec farmers soon found ways of creating land where they could plant crops. They built chinampas – gardens on reclaimed land (see pages 18-19). In these chinampas, farmers grew food for the citizens of Tenochtitlan and also lots of flowers.

Families & Clans

WITHOUT YOUR FAMILY, you would not survive. You need their protection; they give you food, housing, and clothes. If you are a boy, your parents will train you in farming or craft skills; if you are a girl, they will teach you to run a household. You will need family help when you are old or ill. There are no government benefits. Your family's clan, or calpulli (see page 30), oversees your education and makes sure you do not break the law.

Writing in Pictures

THE AZTECS DO not have a written alphabet. So how do they record great events, and preserve their ancient myths and legends? Partly, they train their memories to remember important things. And skilled scribes use picture writing (and pictures for numbers) to keep a detailed record of people and events. Picture writing is carved on stone monuments, and painted on parchment or plant-fiber paper, folded into books.

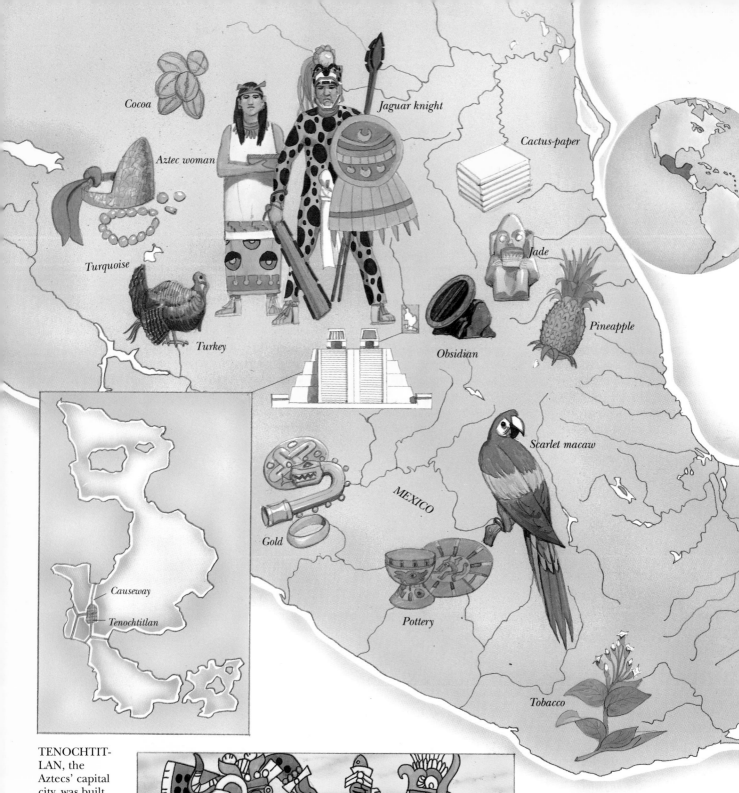

Cocoa

Aztec woman

Jaguar knight

Cactus-paper

Jade

Turquoise

Pineapple

Turkey

Obsidian

Causeway

Tenochtitlan

Scarlet macaw

MEXICO

Gold

Pottery

Tobacco

TENOCHTIT-LAN, the Aztecs' capital city, was built on an island in the middle of Lake Texcoco. It was linked to the mainland by causeways, and surrounded by chinampas. Fresh water was carried to the city from the mountains by a long aqueduct.

(Right) The gods found Tenochtitlan, illustration from a codex.

THE AZTECS believed the world was a beautiful place. Life was hard, but could be joyful, too. After death, most people would suffer. Finally, their souls would fade away, and they would no longer exist. The Aztecs believed that civilization had already been created and destroyed four times. They lived in fear that destruction would occur again. Part of the Aztecs' religion was based on this fear, and on trying to avoid the end of their world.

YOUR MAP OF THE AZTEC WORLD

THE WORLD MAP (left) shows the Aztec lands and their position in Middle America. Many Native American nations were northern neighbors, and lands ruled by the Maya people lay nearby. Much farther south, the Inca people ruled in Peru.

THE BIG PICTURE MAP shows the lands controlled by the Aztecs at the height of their power, about A.D. 1490. It will help you find the places that are mentioned in this book. Aztec influence stretched across a wide area – parts of the present-day countries of Mexico and Guatemala. Within this territory landscape, climate, wildlife, and vegetation varied widely. The map shows you the typical products of each locality. By 1490, all these goods were being claimed by the Aztec rulers as tribute.

BEFORE THE AZTECS became powerful, the Middle American region was inhabited by many different peoples, some rich, some poor, some weak, some strong. They were proudly independent, but they shared many religious beliefs and artistic traditions.

Then, sometime before 1345, the Aztecs arrived from the north; we do not know the precise date. They may perhaps have left their original homeland after it was stricken by drought. At first, they were attacked by the local inhabitants. But the Aztecs were strong, energetic, and ruthless. Soon they took control – and the Aztec empire was founded.

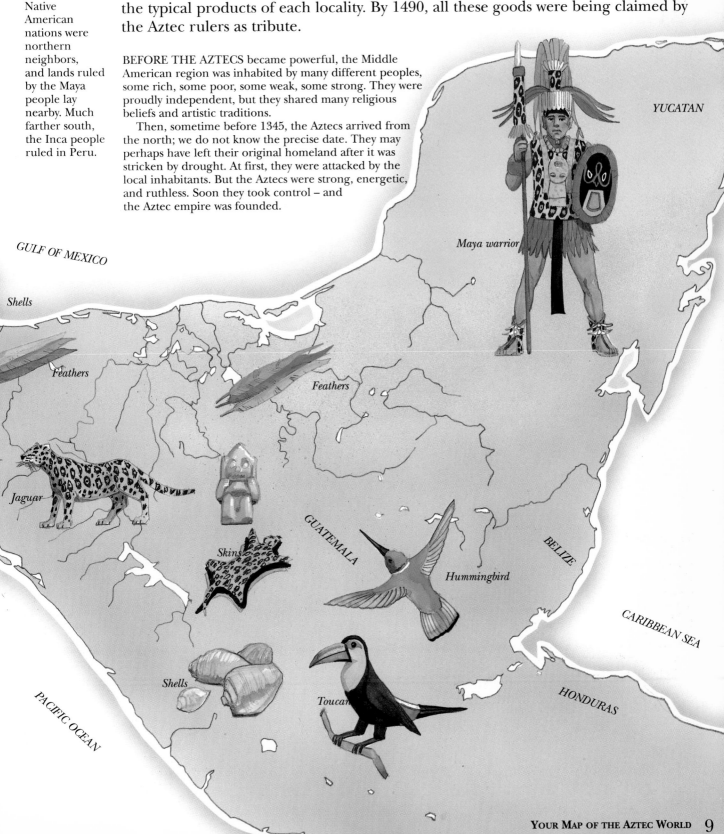

YUCATAN

Maya warrior

GULF OF MEXICO

Shells

Feathers

Feathers

Jaguar

Skins

GUATEMALA

Hummingbird

BELIZE

CARIBBEAN SEA

Shells

Toucan

HONDURAS

PACIFIC OCEAN

BEGIN YOUR NEW LIFE HERE

HERE AND ON the next two pages is a panorama of the world of the Aztecs. It is not meant to be a true-to-life picture, for you would not usually find all these things happening so close together. Its purpose is to act as your guide to this book. Start wherever you wish and follow the Q options.

WHAT IS this building? What is it for?
Go to pages 14-15

HOW DID the Aztecs build their homes?
Go to pages 14-15

WHAT IS this woman making?
Go to pages 20-21

WHAT WAS life like for an Aztec child?
Go to pages 16-17

WHO ARE the men carrying this nobleman on a litter?
Go to pages 31-33

WHAT IS this farmer doing?
Go to pages 18-19

HOW DOES this loom work?
Go to pages 22-23

WHO ARE these men? What might they be carrying?
Go to pages 26-27

WHICH
PLANTS grow
in these farms
and gardens?
Go to pages 18-19

WHAT ARE
these canals
between the
houses?
Go to pages 14-15

ARE THESE
travelers really
spies?
Go to pages 26-27

WHAT
HAPPENS in
these little huts
by the road?
Why were they
built?
Go to pages 18-19

WHAT ARE
these weapons
made of? How
are they used?
Go to pages 32-33

WHY ARE these
men dressed as
animals and
birds?
Go to pages 32-33

WHAT RITUAL is taking place here? *Go to page 29*

HOW DO Aztecs "fly" around the pole? *Go to page 29*

WHAT HAPPENS at the top of all the steps? *Go to pages 36-37*

WHY ARE these buildings so big? *Go to pages 14-15*

WHAT IS this man carrying in his right hand? *Go to pages 32-33*

WHAT ARE these nets and poles for? *Go to pages 20-21*

WHAT HAPPENED to women who died in childbirth? *Go to pages 36-37*

WHAT ANIMALS did the Aztecs hunt? *Go to pages 18-19*

WHY DID ordinary people eat so little meat? *Go to pages 20-21*

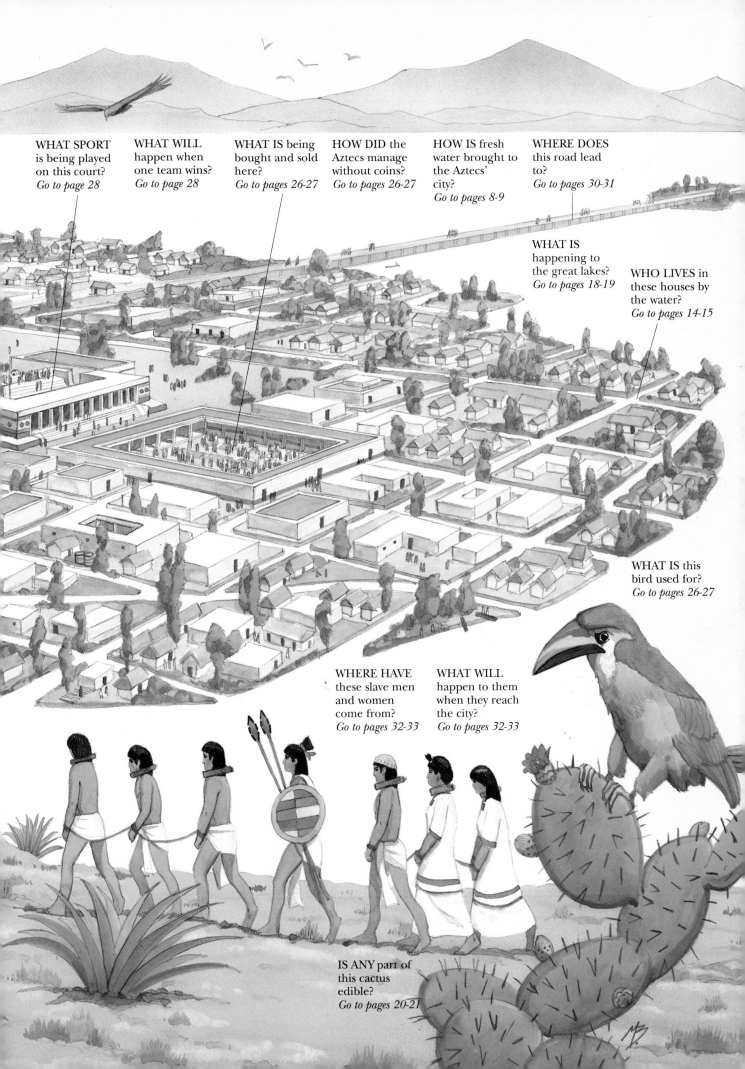

WHAT SPORT is being played on this court? *Go to page 28*

WHAT WILL happen when one team wins? *Go to page 28*

WHAT IS being bought and sold here? *Go to pages 26-27*

HOW DID the Aztecs manage without coins? *Go to pages 26-27*

HOW IS fresh water brought to the Aztecs' city? *Go to pages 8-9*

WHERE DOES this road lead to? *Go to pages 30-31*

WHAT IS happening to the great lakes? *Go to pages 18-19*

WHO LIVES in these houses by the water? *Go to pages 14-15*

WHAT IS this bird used for? *Go to pages 26-27*

WHERE HAVE these slave men and women come from? *Go to pages 32-33*

WHAT WILL happen to them when they reach the city? *Go to pages 32-33*

IS ANY part of this cactus edible? *Go to pages 20-21*

MUD BRICKS

First dig some mud from the riverbed, then mix it with water to make a smooth paste, like dough.

Pack this mixture into a wooden mold. Try to avoid air bubbles; they will make your bricks fragile.

Leave your brick in the hot sun to dry, until it is hard. You will need to make hundreds of bricks for a house.

Finally, you can use your bricks for building. More mud will act as mortar to hold them all together.

AT HOME
WHERE WOULD YOU LIVE?

A S AN AZTEC, where you lived would depend on whether you were rich or poor. (The same is true for most countries today, too.) The Tlatoani and the Cihuacoatl lived in vast stone palaces, with dozens of different rooms, airy courtyards, and beautiful gardens. In the countryside, ordinary people lived in simple mud-brick huts close to their fields. Groups of huts were built in clusters around a village square, for security and companionship.

(Above and left) *How would you store grain to keep it safe from rats? The Aztecs built baked-mud storage bins like these.*

(Below) *The Aztecs did not use chairs. People sat on stools, or on mats on the floor.*

Ladders were made of a thin tree trunk with steps cut in one side.

If you lived in a house thatched with grass and without a chimney, would you dare to light a fire indoors? The Aztecs kept cooking fires safe inside clay pots, like this oven. The legs prevent heat from the fire from scorching mats on the floor.

Q

Now that you have finished cleaning the house, what will you cook for dinner?

Go to pages 20-21

ROOFS AND WALLS

When you have built the walls, you will need to make a roof out of leaves or reeds. For good insulation from heat and cold you need a layer at least 12 inches (30 cm) thick.

Now ask builders to make limewash, to decorate and waterproof the outside of your home. They will dig limestone from the mountainside, then burn it.

It will crumble into powder. The builders will mix this with water and coat the walls. They will add different earths to the limewash to make colored "paint."

You would see very different housing in the island city of Tenochtitlan. Apart from the magnificent palace, ordinary peoples' homes were packed closely together because, as the population grew, land became scarce. Houses were built in neat rows, along carefully planned streets. Most city homes had three or four rooms, simply furnished with rush mats, woven rugs, and clay pots or baskets for storage.

INSIDE THE PALACE

Inside the Tlatoani's palace, you would see statues and wall paintings, a library, a chapel, and separate quarters for his wives and daughters. They spent many hours sewing beautifully embroidered clothes.

The Tlatoani (Aztec leader) received visitors in an impressive hall. They had to bow low before him.

There were peaceful flower gardens – and a noisy zoo – behind the high walls of the palace.

The palace had storerooms for all the tribute goods sent by peoples the Aztecs dominated.

The city of Tenochtitlan was surrounded by water. Houses were built on land that had been reclaimed from the shallow, marshy lake.

In these waterside districts of the city, many of the "streets" were waterways. Citizens traveled to the temples and to market by flat-bottomed canoe.

Scribes kept records of all the goods that arrived, to check that tribute had been paid in full.

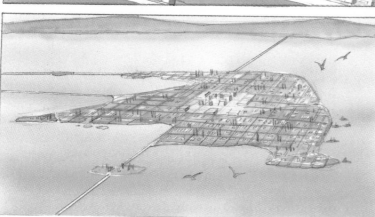

Aztec legends tell how the Aztecs left their homeland after a drought, then wandered in the desert for years. We have no definite evidence of their origins.

They carried statues of their god Huitzilopochtli with them. They believed he would guide them. Legends say that he sent a message in a dream.

The dream message said, "Build your city where you see an eagle with a snake, sitting in a cactus." And this, say the legends, is what they did.

Q

You want some fruit from the prickly pear cactus. Where are they sold?
Go to pages 26-27

YOUR FAMILY
WHO WOULD LIVE WITH YOU?

IF YOU WERE an Aztec boy or girl, you would expect to marry quite young. Between 16 and 20 was the usual age. But if you were a noble's daughter, or a princess, you might be married when you were much younger. It was your duty to marry, to maintain friendly alliances between different peoples in the Aztec-controlled lands. Politically important marriages like this were arranged by the young couple's parents. Ordinary families often arranged their children's marriages, too.

If you were a boy, you would be sent to school. You would specialize in religious studies or Aztec history.

You would also learn to help with essential household tasks, such as collecting fuel for cooking fires.

You would be taught how to handle weapons and how to fight. You need to learn how to be quick and strong.

You would learn to take second place to your parents, grandparents, and all older people.

Q

What weapons would you use if you joined the army?
Go to page 33

(Left and below) *An ordinary family. An Aztec prayer warned them to expect "weariness . . . and weeping" in their life on earth.*

(Above) *A noble Aztec family. They would have slaves and servants to help run their home.*

Aztec laws allowed them to live in bigger, better houses, and to wear fine clothes.

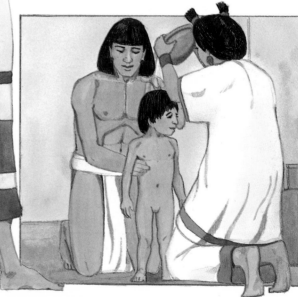

RIGHT AND WRONG

Sixteenth-century Spanish travelers to Aztec lands reported harsh Aztec laws about punishing children. We do not know if they were ever enforced.

These reported punishments varied with age. At 11 or 12, you might be made to breathe smoke from burning chili peppers, or be tied up and left outside all night.

Parents were also responsible for teaching their children various practical skills they would need to support themselves in their adult lives.

Different ranks in Aztec society. **Above**, the Tlatoani.

Cihuacoatl, his assistant and deputy.

Priests and scribes were respected and enjoyed privileges.

Government officials were recruited from noble families.

Men who fought well and bravely became knights.

Farmers and other workers were at the bottom of society.

If you were studious at learning your lessons, you might be accepted to train as a priest. A few girls trained, too.

(Right) The Aztecs had no iron or other useful metals, and no wheeled transportation. Boys born to farming families had to learn to use the foot plow and stone knives. If they were lazy, their parents might punish them.

(Left) People became slaves as captives, as a punishment, or through debt.

You would learn how to study the night sky, and to predict the movements of the planets, the sun, and the moon.

(Above) Slaves for sale, wearing wooden collars.

The collars are a sign that they are unfree.

As in any society, men, women and children were expected to conform to unwritten rules; though not everyone did, of course. A man's role was to work to support his wife and children. His wife's role was to cook, housekeep, and look after everyone else. Since all members of an Aztec family lived together, this might mean anything from nursing an elderly great-grandmother to making sure a crawling baby did not get stung by scorpions. Women also wove clothes and blankets for family use. Children were expected to be hardworking, obedient, and uncomplaining.

Getting married. A bride is carried to the bridegroom's home on the back of a sturdy woman – the matchmaker. At the wedding feast **(below)**, the young couple's clothes are knotted together, as a sign that they will be partners for life.

You might be tattooed with sacred designs. This was a very painful process.

You would learn how to help the priests in the temple, and how to make sacrifices and say prayers.

RUNNING THE HOME

If you were a girl, you would learn from your mother how to spin thread and how to weave cloth using a backstrap loom (see page 23).

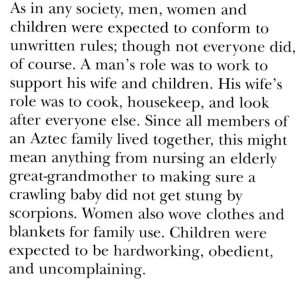

Your mother or grandmother would also teach you how to make tortillas (pancakes) from corn flour, and how to cook meals for the family.

You would be shown how to keep the earth floor of your home clean and tidy, using a broom made of twigs or grass. Boys did not do housework.

Q

You are going to take part in a team game. It could be dangerous. Why?
Go to page 28

FARMING THE LAND
WHAT CROPS WOULD YOU GROW?

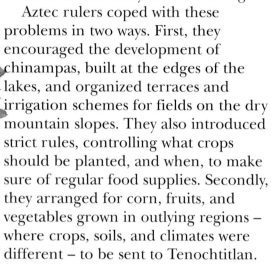

A ZTEC POWER would not have grown so quickly, or have remained so strong, if its rulers had not organized farming and food supplies efficiently. Harvests were always unreliable; droughts or sudden frosts could devastate an entire corn crop. But without corn and vegetables, people would starve. There were not enough "wild" foods – cacti, lizards, rabbits, or sage seeds – to go around. If you were Tlatoani, how would you make sure that everyone had enough to eat?

Aztec rulers coped with these problems in two ways. First, they encouraged the development of chinampas, built at the edges of the lakes, and organized terraces and irrigation schemes for fields on the dry mountain slopes. They also introduced strict rules, controlling what crops should be planted, and when, to make sure of regular food supplies. Secondly, they arranged for corn, fruits, and vegetables grown in outlying regions – where crops, soils, and climates were different – to be sent to Tenochtitlan.

As an Aztec, corn is your main food. It is one of the few cereal crops that can survive the Mexican climate.

You also eat lots of sweet potatoes. The Aztecs did not have white potatoes; they grew in Peru.

Tomatoes ripen quickly in the hot summer months. They are cooked with beans and spices to make stew.

You might also like tasty dishes made with hot chilies and mild sweet peppers, which provide plenty of Vitamin C.

Armadillo

The Aztecs ate many animals unique to the Americas, such as turkeys and armadillos. Turkeys were farmed; the others were hunted.

Rabbit

Turkey

Turtle

Tapir

Strong woven fences stop the muddy chinampa washing away.

CANALS AND CHINAMPAS

You need some new cooking pots. What will you do?
Go to pages 22-23

Water was essential for farming, and also for people to drink. Long canals were cut to carry rainwater from the mountains to villages in the valleys.

You can grow crops like tomatoes and peppers in the fertile chinampas. These are plots of land you have reclaimed from the lake. How did you do this?

First, mark out your plot with posts (above left), then fence it with woven branches. Plant trees all around. Their roots will give support.

Aztec plants:
a. sunflower;
b. carrots; **c.** gourds
and squash;
d. cocoa beans;
e. prickly pear;
f. maguey cactus

The Aztecs farmed their land intensively. Often, this leads to soil exhaustion and a buildup of disease. Heavy manuring stopped soil exhaustion. Plant diseases were controlled by organic methods. *The Aztecs discovered that pests dislike certain types of plants, especially marigolds (Tagetes). They planted them alongside their food crops, and the pests were kept away. Some gardeners are reviving similar "green" techniques today.*

Away from the chinampas, corn and cotton were grown on dry mountain slopes. Manguey cactus was farmed. It gave liquor and fibers for mats, baskets and coarse cloth, paper and needles.

HOW CONVENIENT

You will often find these little wicker buildings beside main roads. They are public toilets.

They are handy for travelers, but even more useful for farmers. Human manure is collected from them each week.

It is loaded into boats, then carried across the lake to the nearest chinampas.

There, you will see it being spread on the fields. It helps to enrich the soil and make the crops grow.

IN A GOOD YEAR, seven separate crops could be grown on a chinampa – one of the most highly productive farming systems ever invented. Chinampas were also used to grow flowers. These were sold in the markets to decorate "mummy bundles" at funerals (see page 35) and nobles' homes.

PLANTING CROPS

Fill your enclosure with mud scooped from the bottom of the lake, plus dead twigs and vegetable scraps. Mix all this together and leave it to rot.

Dig your new ground carefully, using a foot plow. Do not plant any seeds until the government gives orders; otherwise you will be punished.

If you have done your work well, you should find that plants flourish in your chinampa. They like the rich soil and the plentiful water supply.

Q

You are feeling sick and have diarrhea. Whom can you ask for a cure?
Go to pages 34-35

MEALTIMES
WHAT WOULD YOU EAT AND DRINK?

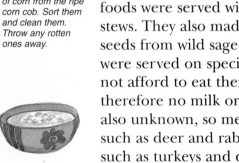

Separate the kernels of corn from the ripe corn cob. Sort them and clean them. Throw any rotten ones away.

Now soak them in limewater. This will help your body to absorb all the nutrition they contain.

Spread the soaked kernels out in the sun. Make sure they dry completely, or else they will soon become moldy.

Grind them between two stones to make coarse flour. This is hard work – your arms may get tired.

FOR ORDINARY PEOPLE, everyday food was simple. Mostly they ate corn, ground into flour and cooked as porridge, tortillas (pancakes), or tamales (stuffed dumplings). These basic plain foods were served with hot, spicy bean and vegetable stews. They also made gruel (like thick soup) out of seeds from wild sage plants (called chia). Meat and fish were served on special occasions; ordinary people could not afford to eat them often. There were no cows, and therefore no milk or cheese. Sheep and horses were also unknown, so meat dishes came from wild animals such as deer and rabbits, or from domesticated animals such as turkeys and dogs.

Aztecs who lived beside the great lakes were able to find many different foods to eat from among lake plants and animals. You might not enjoy some of these – such as grubs and snails – but they were very nourishing. Snacks of crunchy roasted seeds from pumpkins grown on the chinampas might seem nicer.

*Would you eat your dog? The Aztecs bred hairless dogs (**above**) to cook and eat on festival days. They were treated well, but like farm animals, not pets. Aztec dogs did not bark – this was important in a city where 300,000 people lived close together.*

The Aztecs did not use knives and forks; useful metal was too scarce and expensive. Instead, they ate with their fingers, or scooped up soft food with tortillas. They drank from bowls. Men usually ate first; women and children ate later.

MAKING TORTILLAS

Q

Which Aztec gods protect the corn crop?
Go to pages 36 and 43

Mix your corn flour with some cool water to make a sticky dough, but don't get it too wet. Knead it well, then roll it out thinly. Shape it into cakes.

Cook your tortillas on a big pottery dish over an open fire, or in a dome-shaped oven made of clay. Turn them over to brown them on both sides.

Crush chilies for a sauce in this pottery grater – it has a rough, crisscross pattern on the bottom. Serve your sauce in a decorated bowl.

The Aztecs were cannibals; they ate human flesh. But this was never part of ordinary meals. As a rare privilege, flesh from enemy captives killed as sacrifices (see page 32) was shared among the families of warriors who had caught them, although the warriors themselves did not eat it. The flesh was cooked and eaten with corn. These cannibal meals honored the gods. They also reminded everyone that life was perilous and that one day they, too, would die.

Strong beer – called pulque – was made from the maguey cactus. Brewers pulled the central spines out of a mature plant. This left a hole full of sweet, sticky sap. A hollow gourd was secured to the plant, to collect it. When enough sap was collected, it was mixed with old, extra-strong pulque, and left to ferment. People were punished for getting drunk. The Aztecs believed that drunken people were dangerous – evil spirits might enter the city through them. They were also a public nuisance.

Aztec treats come from the deserts and rain forests. They include cocoa beans, used for chocolatl, a chocolate drink.

The prickly pear yields sweet, juicy fruit. Be careful not to hurt yourself on the sharp spines.

Armadillos are a luxury food. Their shells are polished and used to make musical instruments.

Hunger and even starvation might happen during the winter months. This was why it was important for boys to learn to be good hunters. When food was in short supply, poor people lined up for government food rations, or for handouts from wealthy nobles, who held big private feasts at this time.

Spanish travelers claimed the Aztecs had guidelines on how much children should eat. We do not know if they were obeyed. An 8-year-old was allowed one and a half large tortillas per day – plus vegetables, and fish or meat if available. Could you survive on this?

Wild black bees gather nectar from all kinds of flowers. The honey is delicious and the bees don't have stings.

FROM THE LAKE

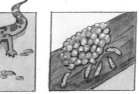

The warm, shallow waters of Lake Texcoco – and the other great lakes nearby – are an ideal breeding ground for fish and turtles and a good source of food.

How would you catch a fish, a frog, or a lizard? The Aztecs used spears and nets. Nets hanging from poles also trapped ducks and geese.

You can find fish eggs, tadpoles, and insect larvae in the scum floating on the lake. The Aztecs think they taste delicious – and they are free!

Q

Why are people sometimes thrown into this lake?

Go to pages 36-37

IN THE WORKSHOPS

WHAT WOULD YOU MAKE?

Craftworking skills were passed on from father to son. Your family might be wood-carvers or carpenters.

Or your father might be a stonemason, who carved gods and skulls to decorate the temples.

You might grow up to be a scribe, who wrote codices (see page 38) for the Aztec government.

Or you might learn the craft of featherwork. The whole family helped with this.

Q

Where can you get brightly colored feathers?
Go to pages 26-27

I F YOU WERE an Aztec worker, you could learn a variety of crafts. You could make fine gold and silver jewelry and amulets, chip sharp-edged knives from flint and obsidian, or carve massive statues out of stone. You could shape clay by hand – the Aztecs did not use potter's wheels – or make mosaics of precious stones. You might even work with feathers; warriors carried feathered shields and standards into battle, as a sign of rank. Aztec rulers valued the shimmering blue-green tail plumage of the rare quetzal bird more highly than gold. Thousands of quetzal feathers were used for headdresses worn by the Tlatoani and other rich nobles.

(Below) Gold buckle, representing the head of the god Xipe Totec. He protected gold-smiths and metal-workers.

(Small pictures, below) Three wonderfully detailed gold ornaments made in Oaxaca, in the southern Aztec lands. They show,

(left to right) an owl, a monkey, and an eagle. According to Aztec law, only noblemen and noblewomen could wear jewels like these.

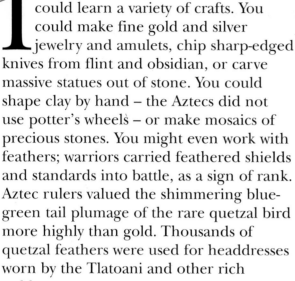

Precious stones, like turquoise (the color of life), were attached to real skulls to make masks.

Metalworkers blow on burning charcoal to make it hot enough to melt gold.

DECORATED SHIELDS

If you want a shield, a skilled Aztec craftsman will make you one. He will cut a strip of bark, then soak it in limewater to soften and preserve it.

He will pound it with a heavy stone hammer, to flatten and spread it. His wife will prepare the feathers. If you want bright colors, she will find them.

The craftsman will draw the pattern you want – perhaps a magic one? – on your shield. Then he will glue the feathers in place, following the pattern.

However, if you really had been born an Aztec, you would have had little choice of career. You would have had to learn the techniques and "trade secrets" your parents taught you. Many craft skills had originated during the Toltec era (A.D. 900 – 1200). The Aztecs learned them when they arrived in Mexico, from descendants of the Toltecs living there. Craftworkers were highly respected, and praised in poems and songs. As one Aztec poet said, "The good artist is wise; God is in his heart."

GOLD AND SILVER

Create delicate gold and silver objects by the lost-wax process. First carve a charcoal model.

(Below) The Aztecs were highly skilled potters. The swirling design on the pot *(a)* represents the wind. The three-legged brazier *(b)* was used for holding fire. The figure on the vase *(c)* is Macuilxochitl, the god of games and feasting.

Making big carvings using simple stone hammers was hard work. This figure of the goddess Coatlicue is over 6½ ft (2 m) high. Its surface was polished by rubbing with sand.

Smear it with wax, let this harden, then cover it with a thick coat of clay. Leave a hole in the clay coat.

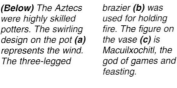

(Above) Hollow pottery statues were shaped in molds, one each for the front and back. Slabs of soft clay were pressed into them, then joined together.

a

b

c

Heat the covered model until the wax melts. Pour this away. Now pour in molten gold or silver; let it cool.

(Below) Ocarinas (whistles), flutes, and toys like this wheeled dog were made from baked clay. Flutes could also be made from bone.

Carefully break open the clay coat. You should find a metal copy of your original model inside.

BACKSTRAP WEAVING

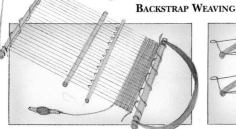

If you want to order a new cloak, an Aztec woman will weave one for you. She will use a simple backstrap loom to produce wonderful patterns.

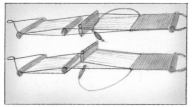

For warp and weft, she will use fibers from the maguey cactus, or, if you can afford it, smooth cotton thread. For winter, she will weave rabbit hair.

She ties the loom to a post, then puts the strap around her waist. This keeps the long warp threads taut and lets her pass the short weft threads between them.

Q

What happened to many of the finest gold and silver items made by the Aztecs?
Go to pages 42-43

YOUR CLOTHES

WHAT WOULD YOU WEAR?

If you were a man, you would wear a loincloth, often tied at the front with an elaborate bow.

Then you would put on your cloak. This might be decorated with woven patterns or embroidery.

Your cloak fastens on one shoulder, leaving your strongest hand free.

I F YOU WERE an Aztec, you would be able to tell a great deal about someone – their rank in society, their military duties, their place in the government, and how rich or poor they were – just by looking at their clothes. Cloaks, headdresses, jewels, uniforms, and face paints all gave instantly recognizable information about the people who wore them. Fine clothes and jewels were a sign of status. They were extremely valuable; only nobles and a few rich merchants could afford them. A well-dressed Aztec noble could advertise his wealth by parading in public. Noblewomen mostly stayed at home, so only their families saw their fine clothes. On special occasions, they liked to use makeup (yellow face paint and a red tint for lips and teeth), but their husbands and fathers disapproved.

Mirror made of obsidian – a glassy rock formed when volcanoes erupt. The frame is carved from wood.

(Above) Gold ring decorated with a bird's head.
(Below) Gold brooch shaped like a shield, inlaid with turquoise and hung with bells.

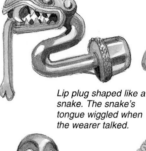

Lip plug shaped like a snake. The snake's tongue wiggled when the wearer talked.

(Above) A fine gold/copper pectoral (chest ornament).

The grim head portrays the spirit of death and darkness.

(Above) Gold earring in the shape of a death's-head.

If you were a soldier, you might wear a helmet; if you were a noble, you might have a fine headdress.

WHAT YOUR CLOTHES SAY ABOUT YOU

Maguey cactus provides leaf-tip "needles" and leaf-fiber "thread".

Sandals like these are worn only by the rich; the poor go barefoot.

In summer, the well-dressed Aztec noble always uses his feather fan.

Ordinary soldiers wear plain, simple tunics made of quilted cotton.

If you capture many enemies, you might be promoted to be a jaguar knight.

If you are made an officer, you will wear even more splendid clothes.

Q

What would you grow to be sure you could have some new clothes?
Go to pages 18-19

The strict rules about Aztec clothes and jewelry separated rich from poor, nobles from ordinary people. Only nobles could wear clothes made from feathers and soft, silky cotton, or jewels made of precious metals and stones. Ordinary citizens' clothes were woven from the rough fibers of the maguey cactus. And ordinary men could not wear long, flowing cloaks, unless the legs had been badly scarred in war.

Fine clothing was given to warriors as a reward for bravery. Hosts also gave it to nobles attending their banquets. Gift-giving like this was a sign of the giver's wealth and power, not his generosity.

If you were a woman, you would wear a long, loose skirt.

(Left) Gold jewelry: **a.** circular pins; **b.** eagle-beaked pendant; **c.** necklace, and **d.** earrings. Jewelry like this would be worn by noblemen. Aztec men were more elaborately dressed than women.

(Below) A procession of noblemen and warriors, dressed in their best. Their clothing is made from luxury materials: cotton, feathers, skins, and fur, and ornamented with embroidery and semiprecious stones. They are carrying shields, standards, sunshades, and bunches of flowers.

Eagle knight – a high-ranking noble – wearing a uniform decorated with feathers.

Then you would put on a baggy over-tunic, decorated with embroidery.

You would arrange your hair, and fasten it with woven braids.

Then, if you were noble, you might add a necklace of turquoise and gold.

Boys who have not killed enemies must wear their back hair long, like girls.

Soldiers wear topknots; it is a sign that they are brave, adult men.

Unmarried girls leave their long hair flowing over their shoulders.

Married women tie their long hair in bunches or braids, like this.

Soldiers wear face paint to look impressive and to frighten the enemy.

Priests paint their faces with sacred patterns, full of religious meaning.

Q

Why has everyone been dancing all night?
Go to pages 36-37

AT THE MARKET

WHAT WOULD YOU BARTER, BUY, AND SELL?

You want to buy something. What valuable goods could you offer in exchange? Try cocoa beans. No good?

Then what about some gold dust? This is worth much more. The best way to carry it is inside hollow quills.

Could you exchange something you have made for what you want to buy? Try bargaining, and see if it works.

If you are poor, you can offer to work for several days in return for the goods you want.

Are the two men (above) just gossiping? Perhaps they are merchants or spies. Travel was slow and risky in Aztec lands, and merchants were the only people who traveled regularly. So the Aztec government often asked them to make reports on what they had seen on their journeys. For this reason, some people said merchants were spies.

B Y ABOUT 1450, the population of Tenochtitlan numbered at least 300,000. An enormous amount of food and other goods were needed to provide for all these people, and a vast market grew up on the nearby island of Tlatelolco. At first it was independent, but, after a riot, it was conquered by Aztec soldiers in 1473. Local trade was women's work. City women went to market almost every day to trade food they had cooked or cloth they had woven for corn, vegetables, pottery, mats, and baskets. The Aztecs had no coins, so goods were bartered (traded).

TRANSPORT AND TRADE

Q

You are a market official. Who organizes your work?
Go to pages 30-31

If you are a wealthy merchant, you will hire porters to carry the goods you are buying or selling to and from the markets in big cities in the Aztecs' lands.

The porters are very strong; they carry everything on their backs. Bundles are slung from a tumpline – a band of cloth – across their foreheads and over their shoulders.

Aztecs know how wheels work, but many tracks are too steep for wheeled traffic to use. On the many lakes canoes are the best means of transportation.

AZTEC NUMBERS

1 20 400 8,000

The Aztecs used picture symbols for writing numbers. You can see some of them here.

Could you write like a scribe? Using Aztec picture symbols (all on this page) write: 1 box of beans; 20 baskets of chilies.

How would you write: 400 boxes of cotton or 8,000 shields? Would you like to be a scribe?

Longer-distance trade was risky, and was controlled by Aztec merchants. They traveled over snowy mountain passes and along rough, rocky tracks. They faced hostile people, wild animals, poisonous spiders, and snakes. There were a few shelters, but Aztec people were discouraged, by law, from welcoming strangers to their homes. Not surprisingly, merchants charged high prices.

AS MANY AS 20,000 people might have visited the market each day. Trade was governed by strict laws. Anyone stealing or cheating would be tried on the spot. If guilty, they could be beaten to death. Many smaller markets were held in villages and towns. People walked to them from the countryside nearby. Like the market at Tlatelolco, they were places to meet friends, enjoy gossip, and watch the world go by.

Rare and exotic creatures were also sent to the Tlatoani as tribute; this bird is for his private zoo.

RICH TRIBUTES

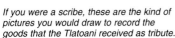

a   b   c   d   e   f

If you were a scribe, these are the kind of pictures you would draw to record the goods that the Tlatoani received as tribute.

(Left to right) a. fine cloaks; b. clothes for warriors; c. shields; d. box of cotton; e. box of beans; f. baskets of chilies.

If these tribute goods were perishable, the Tlatoani and the nobles sold what they could not use themselves, before it went bad.

Q

Why did conquered peoples keep on sending this tribute?
Go to pages 32-33

FESTIVALS

HOW WOULD YOU CELEBRATE?

CROCODILE
Around the borders of these pages are 20 symbols for the names of the days used in the Aztecs' holy calendar.

WIND
The Aztecs used three different calendars to measure time; this one was used by priests and scribes.

HOUSE
It was called tonalpohualli. According to this holy calendar, there were 13 months in a year.

LIZARD
There were 20 days in each month, so the year according to the Aztecs' holy calendar was 260 days long.

TO THE AZTECS, the world was a threatening place, ruled by powerful, unseen forces that controlled the weather, the seasons, and even time itself. If you wanted to survive, you could not ignore them. If they were disturbed or offended, the world might collapse in chaos. So, the Aztecs developed many elaborate festivals to link their lives as closely as possible with the life-giving forces that shaped their world. Festivals and rituals kept the world running smoothly, and kept time from coming to an end.

(Right) Tlachtli was as exciting, risky team sport. Players tried to hit a heavy rubber ball through stone hoops fixed high on the court wall, using only their elbows and hips; often, they got badly bruised. Winning teams could demand all the spectators' clothes and jewels; losing teams might be sacrificed to the gods. Ball-game courts **(below)** were large – over 165 feet (50 m) long and 33 feet (10 m) wide.

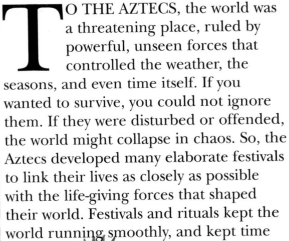

Ball-game court.

(Left) The new Fire ceremony, held once every 52 years, when two of the Aztecs' three calendars, the count of days and the farmers' calendar (see page 39), ended at much the same time. All fires were put out, and people waited while priests watched the sky for the first sight of the Pleiades stars. If they appeared, the world would not end. Then a man was sacrificed and a fire was lit in his chest. Bundles of sticks were held there until they kindled, and the new fire was carried to homes throughout the land.

NAMES OF DAYS

SNAKE   **DEATH'S-HEAD**
This holy calendar was used by priests and scribes to compile the Aztecs' sacred Book of Days.

DEER   **RABBIT**
They used the Book of Days to foretell the future. Some days would be good, others evil.

WATER   **DOG**
Different days were protected by different gods. Each one decided what happened on their days.

Q

How would you measure time if you were an Aztec farmer?
Go to pages 38-39

Some festivals featured sacrifices, somber and bloodthirsty, designed to "feed" the supernatural forces and give them (and the Aztecs) continued life. Other festivals were full of energy and celebration, and linked to sports or games. They encouraged the world to go on existing by imitating natural events. For example, the movements of the ball in the game of tlachtli represented the sun's path across the sky.

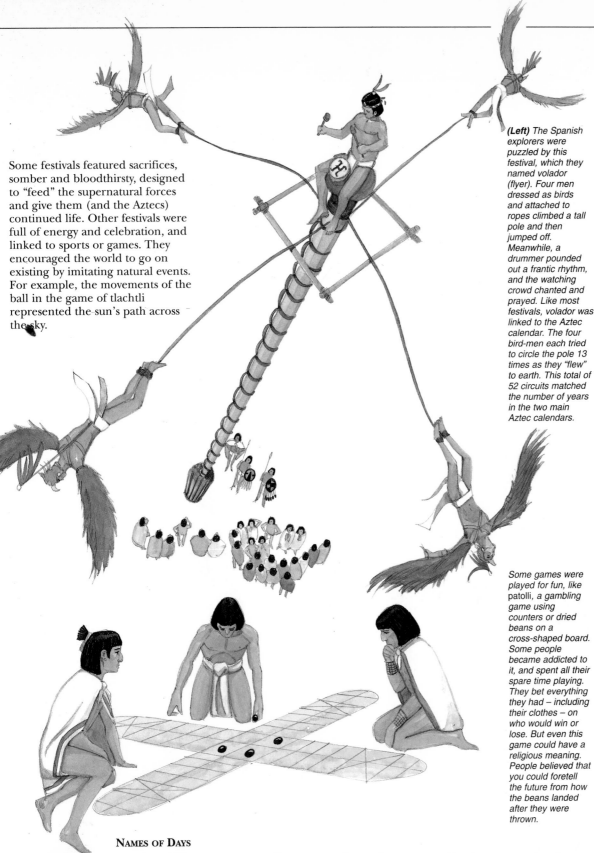

(Left) The Spanish explorers were puzzled by this festival, which they named volador (flyer). Four men dressed as birds and attached to ropes climbed a tall pole and then jumped off. Meanwhile, a drummer pounded out a frantic rhythm, and the watching crowd chanted and prayed. Like most festivals, volador was linked to the Aztec calendar. The four bird-men each tried to circle the pole 13 times as they "flew" to earth. This total of 52 circuits matched the number of years in the two main Aztec calendars.

FLOWER
These calendar names for days were important in another way, too.

RAIN
Babies were often named after the day and month when they were born.

FLINT KNIFE
Names such as One Jaguar or Four Rain were common. Would you like a name like this?

Some games were played for fun, like patolli, a gambling game using counters or dried beans on a cross-shaped board. Some people became addicted to it, and spent all their spare time playing. They bet everything they had – including their clothes – on who would win or lose. But even this game could have a religious meaning. People believed that you could foretell the future from how the beans landed after they were thrown.

MOVEMENT
Aztecs believed that the day you were born affected your character and destiny.

MONKEY   GRASS
The holy calendar can help us find out about the Aztecs' everyday lives. How can it do this? Imagine you are an Aztec.

REED   JAGUAR
What events are most important in your life? What creatures and objects do you see all around?

EAGLE   VULTURE
You will choose these as the names for the days of your calendar, because everyone will recognize them easily.

Q

You have a bad cough, but none of your friends or family has it; what can have caused it?
Go to pages 34-35

GOVERNMENT
WHO WOULD RULE YOUR LIFE?

Noble visitors meet all these in the palace: Cihuacoatl with his bodyguards;

AZTEC GOVERNMENT was strong and well organized. Sixteenth-century Europeans in Tenochtitlan commented, "It is astonishing to see the order and good government that is maintained everywhere." The Tlatoani, helped by nobles and army commanders, was in charge. At home, he organized massive building and road repair projects, arranged food and water supplies, controlled farms and markets, played an important part in religious rituals, and administered the law. Abroad, the first Tlatoanis made friendly alliances with nearby states; later Tlatoanis forced them to co-operate through fear of Aztec power.

Scribes recording their Tlatoani's history;

Cooks, cleaners, porters, body-guards, and zoo-keepers;

(Left) *Aztec rulers used messengers to send instructions to officials in distant conquered lands. There were roads linking major conquered towns with Tenochtitlan, but no wheeled transportation. Messengers had to travel everywhere on foot. Messages were carried in forked sticks.*

CALPULLIS – clans based on shared ancestry and neighborhoods – controlled local law and order, and provided education and emergency help for their members, as well. Ordinary Aztecs, and peoples in allied states, were kept under control by the threat of punishment. Even the rules about Aztec clothing made sure that everyone "knew their place." Aztec rulers believed this strict control was essential if they were to keep power.

(Left) *If you were an Aztec ruler, you would keep soldiers and nobles loyal to you by rewarding men who had served you well. There was a scale of rewards for taking prisoners, for example. A warrior who captured two would receive a cloak with an orange border. If he captured four, he would receive a jaguar suit.*

(Left) *Messengers also acted as spies. Dressed in padded cotton armor, they traveled by night, exploring enemy lands. They carried a conch-shell trumpet (below) to sound the alarm if they were caught.*

Tumblers, acrobats, musicians, and dancers.

AZTEC RULERS (TLATOANI)

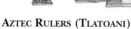

Q

You come from an ordinary family and there is talk of war. Your parents are excited. Why?
Go to pages 32-33

Acamapichtli (1367-1395)

Huitzilihuitl (1396-1417)

Chimalpopoca (1417-1427)

Izcoatl (1427-1440)

Montezuma I (1440-1469)

Axayacatl (1469-1481)

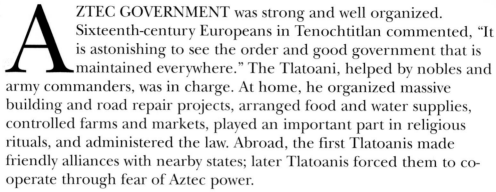

If you are caught committing a crime, you will be brought before a judge. No excuses are allowed.

(Left) The Tlatoani meets leading nobles and warriors to discuss future campaigns. He sits on the raised porch of one of the rooms in his palace, while the council members sit on mats in the courtyard outside.

You might be kept prisoner in a cage. For a first crime, you will be set free, or your house will be knocked down.

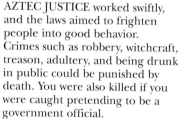

But if you are caught again, you will be strangled. Or you could be made a slave, or chosen for sacrifice.

(Left) Bribes might be used, as well as gifts or threats, to force nearby rulers to become the Aztecs' allies.

(Above) Head-dress made of quetzal feathers and gold, once owned by the Tlatoani Montezuma.

AZTEC JUSTICE worked swiftly, and the laws aimed to frighten people into good behavior. Crimes such as robbery, witchcraft, treason, adultery, and being drunk in public could be punished by death. You were also killed if you were caught pretending to be a government official.

Old people were not punished for some crimes, like drunkenness. But young people were clubbed to death.

*Tizoc
(1481-1486)*

*Ahuitzotl
(1486-1502)*

*Montezuma II
(1502-1520)*

*Hernan Cortés
(Spanish conqueror)*

*Cuitlahuac
(1520)*

*Cuauhtemoc
(1520-1525)*

Q

Everyone is tense and nervous. You are not allowed to sleep. Why?
Go to pages 38-39

WARS AND CONQUESTS

WHO WOULD BE YOUR ENEMIES? WHOM WOULD YOU FIGHT?

As a jaguar knight you might be sent on secret fighting missions at night. You would send signals by whistling.

If you were an eagle knight, you would be trained to make surprise raids at dawn.

Eagle knights lived in special quarters near the Great Temple (see page 36), where they held special festivals.

As a soldier, you had a chance to win status and respect. It was the only way ordinary men might become nobles.

IF YOU WERE AN AZTEC BOY, it would be your destiny and your duty to fight. Newborn boy babies were greeted with a poem praising their future bravery in battle. At school, boys were trained to use weapons, and at eighteen they were taken to watch real fighting. Then they had to join the next war. They were organized into groups of six; each group was expected to take at least one captive. When they did, the captive was killed and his body cut up and shared between them. They took their share home to their families to prove they were now "real men."

This system of training shows the Aztecs were always ready for war. They relied on winning new land and keeping control of conquered cities. Without tribute from defeated enemies, the Aztecs could not maintain their way of life.

Once a year, specially chosen captives were sacrificed in a ritual contest (**below**). Beforehand, they were treated well. Then they were tied to a stone, and armed with wood and feather weapons. Senior knights slowly killed them. As their blood flowed, it was meant to nourish the earth.

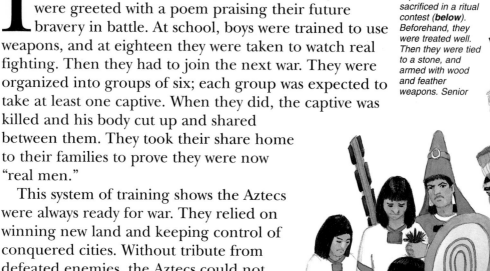

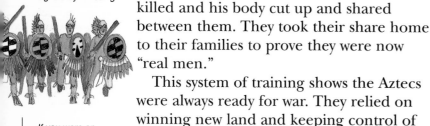

IN 1428, the Aztecs formed a Triple Alliance with two powerful neighbor states. But this did not bring peace. Before long, the Aztecs declared war on Tlaxcala. Perhaps they did not aim to conquer; certainly they wanted captives to sacrifice. In Aztec poetry, "flowers" meant "blood," and these wars were known as the Flowery Wars.

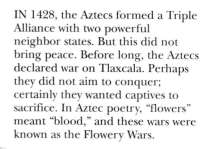

AZTEC CONQUESTS

Q

What happened to Aztec soldiers killed in battle?
Go to pages 36-37

When the Aztecs wanted to conquer a city, they sent ambassadors.

They usually asked for a "treaty of friendship" and a present of gold.

The city leaders had 20 days to decide what to do. Refusal meant war.

Meanwhile, the Aztecs made preparations for battle.

The ambassadors returned, to ask what decision had been made.

Back home, Aztec soldiers were told to leave their homes and families.

(Left) Warriors from different states used different weapons. This bowman from Tlaxcala has arrows tipped with flint. Aztec warriors attached dead women's fingers to their armor as charms to protect them from injury.

(Left) the Aztecs used knives like these to cut the hearts out of captives taken in war. Two, *a* and *c*, have "demon faces." They are made of flint; *b* is decorated with mosaic.

(Below) Battles were fought on foot. It was a deep disgrace to run away. Troops from the Otomi people (who lived north of the Aztecs) vowed never to step backward in battle, but always to advance. The Aztecs' clubs, edged with razor-sharp flakes of obsidian, caused terrible injuries.

AFTER THE CONQUEST

The Aztecs did not keep garrisons in conquered cities; surviving Aztec troops came home.

Conquered cities were made to provide rich tribute; if they did not, they were punished severely.

An Aztec noble or army commander was appointed governor of the conquered city.

Captives had to work as slaves, or else they might be sacrificed. Being sacrificed could be an honor.

AZTEC CONQUESTS

If the city refused the treaty, Aztec priests chose when the war began.

The Aztec army assembled in battle formation in the Temple Precinct.

A huge task force set out to attack the city – now the enemy.

Each army unit marched separately, led by proud standard-bearers.

They had to conquer the enemy city, or else they would get no food.

Army discipline was strict. If soldiers disobeyed orders, they were killed.

Q You need spies to help you get to know enemy territory. Whom will you send?
Go to pages 26-27

SICKNESS AND HEALTH
WHAT WOULD HAPPEN IF YOU FELT ILL?

If you were ill, how would you try to get better? You could take medicines made from herbs.

Or you could put your trust in magic charms and amulets like these.

FOR THE AZTECS, medicine was a mixture of practical knowledge, religious belief, and magic. An Aztec doctor, or *ticitl*, had a vast number of treatments to choose from when trying to cure patients. These ranged from simple first aid learned from soldiers on the battlefield, herbal medicines (the Aztecs recognised over 1,200 effective medicinal plants), and steam baths to fortune telling, prayers, and spells. Men and women could be doctors; but only women became midwives, or healers with (the Aztecs believed) special powers to remove stones from the body or worms from the eyes.

The treatments doctors chose depended on what they believed the cause of the disease to be.

(Below) *Medicinal plants:* **a.** *tobacco* **b.** *psilocybin mushrooms* **c.** *peyote* **d.** *morning glory*

Aztecs used the dangerous mind-altering drugs found in these plants to help diagnosis. They belived that the drugged patient made contact with the spirit world, and learned the cause of their illness.

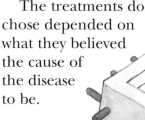

Perhaps a special diet might help. When the Aztecs were ill, they stopped eating meat.

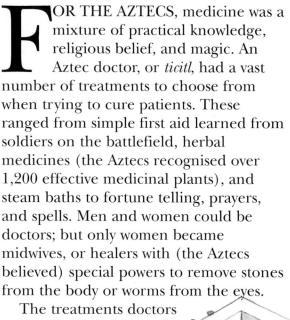

Or you might fast – that is, give up food altogether for several days.

STEAM BATHS were mud-brick houses with a furnace outside one wall. Patients sat inside, a fire was lit in the furnace, then water was poured over the red-hot inner wall. It turned into steam, surrounding the patients and making them sweat. Aztec doctors prescribed steam baths for a wide variety of illnesses, including aching joints, colds, and chills. Steam baths were also used to purify people taking part in religious rituals.

FAITH HEALING

Q

Who would make a magic amulet for you?
Go to pages 22-23

If you were an Aztec, you believed the gods could cure you. Holy water was stored in some temples, ready to sprinkle on sick children.

Gods sent diseases: Amimitl caused coughs, and Tlaloc caused ulcers. You might persuade them to cure you by making offerings of food.

The gods might listen to your prayers. They might also speak to you (and your doctor) in dreams. Or they might decide it was time for you to die.

According to Aztec medical theory, similar symptoms might be caused by very different ills. The patient might have broken a religious rule, or offended one of the gods. An enemy might have sent an invisible "weapon" to poison the patient's body, or the patient might have met a ghost.

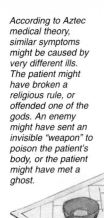

Aztec doctor treating patient by divination.

Aztec doctors used divination to look into the future. A bundle of strings was thrown on the ground. If one string fell away from the others, then the patient would get better. If not he would die.

DO NOT TRY ANY OF THE AZTEC REMEDIES OR TREATMENTS SHOWN IN THIS BOOK. THEY COULD BE VERY DANGEROUS

FUNERALS

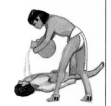

What happened when you died? First, an offering of water was poured over your corpse.

Then the undertakers (usually, old men) arranged your body in a sitting position, like this.

(Right) Aztec people were at risk from poisonous **a**. scorpions **b**. ants **c**. spiders.

(Below left) Mummy bundles **a**. shown in a codex drawing; **b**. artist's reconstruction

They wrapped you carefully in cloth, to make a mummy bundle. Then they killed a dog, and put it on your lap.

TO MODERN EYES, Aztec ideas about what caused disease look unscientific. Yet some Aztec treatments definitely worked. Certain herbs, like pennyroyal, used for catarrh did (and still do) have healing powers. Aztec doctors knew how to splint broken limbs and sew up cuts with human hair. Other Aztec treatments were dangerous, and, perhaps because of them, patients died. But even dying patients were encouraged by feeling that doctors were doing all they could to help. And, as the Aztecs' religion taught, everyone's fate was decided by the gods.

They decorated your mummy bundle with feathers and flowers, and jewels, too, If you were rich. Then it was buried or burned.

TOOTH CARE

As a child, you would be told to clean your teeth with salt and charcoal mixed together.

For a toothache, use a poultice of pine resin (which kills bacteria) and worms.

If this doesn't work, hold a hot chili against the painful tooth. This will help to numb it.

To relieve painful gums, prick them. This was very dangerous; it spread bacteria.

If all else fails, the tooth must be pulled out. Use strong thread and give a sharp tug.

Fill the cavity with salt. This will help to reduce the risk of infection afterwards.

Q

Where did your soul go after you were dead?
Go to page 37

Go to page 37

YOUR BELIEFS

WHAT WOULD YOU HOPE FOR AND FEAR?

Aztec priests offering sacrifices of blood to the gods, from a codex.

I T IS A WARM, DARK NIGHT. Along with thousands of other men and women, you are dancing outside the Great Temple. You are exhausted, but also happy and excited, because you are taking part in a religious ritual. You are helping your people, the Aztecs, to survive.

The Aztecs believed that because the earth nourished them with its "flesh" of crops and water, they must offer their own flesh and the "precious water" of blood in return. The gods had suffered when creating the world, so human pain was needed for the world to continue. The tears of sacrificed small children, for example, made sure the rain would fall. Young men were sacrificed to Chalchiuhtlicue, goddess of the lake waters.

THE AZTECS worshiped over 60 different gods, but they were really just different views of one supreme power. Some, like the earth goddess Toci (Our Grandmother) or Xilonen (goddess of corn), represented forces of nature, and were honored in many parts of America. Others were the Aztecs' own tribal spirits. Many were remote, cruel, and unpredictable. Only Quetzalcoatl – a legendary priest-king – was praised for his gentleness, and offered sacrifices of flowers, not blood.

Temple sacrifices reminded Aztecs of ancient myths and legends about the sufferings of their ancestors.

Long ago, the legends said, your ancestors were tired and hungry in the desert. They had no home.

So they made human sacrifices to Huitzilopochtli, their god, to ask for his help.

He led them to Mexico, where they settled and grew strong. They built a big temple to honor him.

(Right) The Great Temple in Tenechtitlan, sacred to Tlaloc (the rain god) and Huitzilopochtli, the Aztecs' main god. Victims were sacrificed at twin altars at the top of the steps. Priests cut open victims' chests, and held their hearts up to the sky, where the gods lived. Blood ran down the temple steps, or was smeared on the walls. The smell was terrible. Victims' bodies were eaten as holy meals, or fed to animals in the Tlatoani's zoo.

(Right) Turquoise pectoral like a two headed snake sacred to Quetzalcoatl, who would one day return to signal the end of the world.

A PRIEST'S LIFE

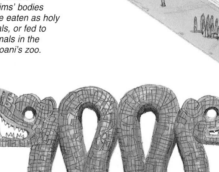

Q

You want to learn to play a musical instrument. Which one?
Go to pages 22-23

As a priest, you will need: pottery burner for copal (fragrant incense);

Bag for copal – used in temples to disguise the smell of blood;

Sharp cactus spikes, to produce drops of your blood to offer to the gods;

Tobacco to smoke or chew to help you keep awake during all-night vigils.

You can train as a priest if you are willing to work hard. You will go to calmecac (school) to study religion, law, and mathematics, and help the priests in temple ceremonies.

(Left) Mictlanteuctli, god of the dead. Aztecs believed that after death, most souls went on a long, painful journey until they reached a place called Mictlan. Then they stopped existing. They found peace at last in utter nothingness. But souls of heroes and sacrifice victims lived in heaven with the sun god.

Not all souls found rest. Some returned to earth as ghosts, like women who died in childbirth or the headless Night Ax, which stalked the streets with a gaping wound in its chest, ready to eat anyone it met.

Aztec priest at a sacrifice

DEATH'S-HEADS

As an Aztec, you would see images of death all around your city. This skull mask is made of obsidian.

Masks were also made in skull shape, like this one, of cedarwood and turquoise.

Stone statues of gods and goddesses might be carved with a skull, instead of a face.

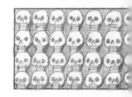

Huge skull racks stood outside Aztec temples. Some were carved decorations, others held real human skulls.

If you have a good voice, you can be trained to sing – music is an important part of many ceremonies. Or you might learn to play bone flutes, shell trumpets, rattles, or big drums.

If you are good at mathematics, you will learn to calculate and observe the movements of the planets and the stars, and to predict storms, comets, and eclipses.

You will find some parts of the priests' training very hard. You may have to chant prayers all night and learn endurance by standing in icy mountain pools.

Q

Where could you find fine jade, turquoise, and obsidian?
Turn to pages 8-9

ALTHOUGH MOST AZTEC people could not read or write, keeping accurate, detailed records was very important. As one noble proudly claimed: "The Aztecs had scribes for all areas of knowledge. Some wrote histories, others genealogies, some noted boundaries of cities and villages and fields . . . some made law books . . . priests wrote down everything to do with temples . . . and learned men drew pictures of all their discoveries."

Scribes and priests also devised calendars to measure time. The Aztecs lived in fear that their world might end. They believed this had happened four times before, and that their own world was the fifth, and final, new creation. If it ended, it could not be born again. Everything would be destroyed, forever.

If you were a scribe, you could choose different ways of writing. Drawing pictures was simplest.

Or you might draw patterns or symbols to show difficult ideas. For example, this represents the sun god.

tlantli (teeth)

tepeti (mountain)
Most pictures, like these, had one main meaning. But they could also be used like letters, to spell words.

Tepetitlan

The pictures above mean "teeth" and "mountain". Put them together and they sound like a city's name: Tepetitlan.

Q

Why did Tlatoani Itzcoatl (1427-1440) burn all the early Aztec codices?
Go to page 45

Scribes wrote with a brush using black ink and brilliant colored paints.

(Above) *Aztec paper was made from maguey cactus fibers or fig-tree bark. Almost half a million sheets of fig-bark paper were sent to scribes in Tenochtitlan every year, as tribute.*

CODICES

If you want to learn about your nation's history, you will have to learn to read codices or listen to recitals from them. Codices are magnificent folding books produced by Aztec scribes.

Codices are a combination calendar and history book; they record the lives of priests and kings, laws, wars, tributes, and the movements of the stars. Some codices show scenes of Aztec life.

It takes a lot of time to write a codex, and also to read one. The information is arranged zigzag across each page, in a series of picture stories. It is easy to lose you place, so you'll need to concentrate.

The Aztecs had three main calendars. The two most important were the holy calendar, with years of 260 days, and the farmers' calendar, with years of 365 days. Aztec priests also used a third calendar, based on the movements of the planet Venus. Each Venus year had 584 days. Once every 52 years (52 x 365 days) the holy calendar year and the farmers' calendar year ended within five days of each other. During this period, the Aztecs thought the world might end.

These five days were a time of great danger. Priests anxiously held the New Fire ceremony (see page 28). Everyone stayed indoors, doing as little as possible. People wore masks made of cactus leaves to hide themselves from the powerful forces that ruled heaven and earth. Pregnant women were watched; if the world was going to end, they would be taken over by evil spirits and devour their families. Children were kept awake; if they fell asleep, they might turn into mice.

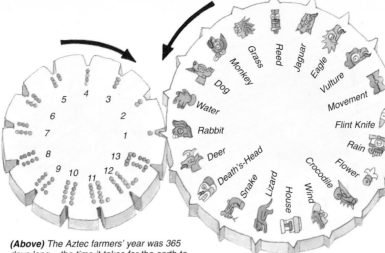

(Above) The Aztec farmers' year was 365 days long – the time it takes for the earth to travel around the sun. Farmers' crops needed the sun's warmth to grow. The farmers' year had 18 months, each of 20 days, plus 5 days extra. The months' names are given below. Each month had special festivals, when the gods were worshiped.

(Below) The Sun Stone, found in Tenochtitlan, dates from about 1480.

(Above) The Aztec holy calendar. The two wheels show how its 20 days are counted to make up its 13 months. A year ends when the small wheel has made one complete turn, and the big wheel has made 13 complete turns. After 18,980 days, 73 holy years and 52 farmers' years end together.

YEAR BEARERS

a House

Aztec 365-day years always ended on one of the four days shown here: *a.* House *b.* Rabbit *c.* Reed *d.* Flint Knife.

b Rabbit

These days were called Year Bearers. The year they began was recorded by scribes like this: "In the year Rabbit."

c Reed

To avoid confusion between recent years with the same name, the Aztecs numbered them over the 52-year cycle.

d Flint Knife

So years were known as 1-13 House, 1-13 Rabbit, 1-13 Reed, 1-13 Flint Knife. As you can see, dots were used for numbering.

The Sun Stone records Aztec beliefs about time and the world's past

creations. Each creation was called a "sun" and was named after the force

that had destroyed it – Jaguar, Wind, Water, Rain: (1) first creation, Jaguar; (2)

second creation, Wind; (3) third creation, Rain; (4) fourth creation,

Water; (5) pictures of the names of the days in the holy calendar; (6) sun's

face (or, possibly, the face of the earth god – historians are not certain).

THE FARMERS' YEAR

February - March
1 End of the Rains
2 Month of Flaying
3 Short Vigil

April - May
4 Long Vigil
5 Drought
6 Bean Porridge

June - July
7 Lesser Lords' Feast
8 Great Lords' Feast
9 Offering Flowers

August - September
10 Ripe Fruits
11 Sweeping Up
12 Return of Gods

October - November
13 Mountain Feast
14 Month of Birds
15 Feather Banners

December - January
16 Rain Begins
17 Winter
18 Growing Starts

Q

Why were the Aztecs fightened by the Spanish?
Go to pages 40-41

END OF THE EMPIRE

HOW WOULD YOU DEFEND YOUR LAND?

Imagine how Montezuma felt when messengers told him they had seen mountains floating on the sea.

They also said they had seen strange, metal-amored creatures, "half man, half deer."

Would you do as Montezuma did, and send friendly ambassadors to greet them?

Would you believe it when messengers reported that these strange monsters had weapons that shot fire?

Q

Why did the Aztecs not realize that the Spaniards were riding horses?
Go to pages 20-21

Cortés and his soldiers arrived as conquerors, not as friends.

EVER SINCE 1509, reports of monstrous creatures, mysterious fires, and ghostly voices had reached Tlatoani Montezuma. He consulted the priests. "The future has already been decided by the gods," they replied. Montezuma remembered an ancient prophecy. One day, the Toltec priest-king Quetzalcoatl would return. Then, in spite of all the Aztecs' prayers and sacrifices, the world would end. What should he do to save his people?

In 1519, news came that strangers had landed. Were they Quetzalcoatl's servants? Were they monsters or gods? Faced with this uncertainty, Montezuma did what he could. He greeted the newcomers with dignity, and welcomed them to Tenochtitlan. But the strangers were Spaniards, seeking gold. Within a year, they controlled the city, and Montezuma was dead. By 1521, the Spaniards had seized power and two hundred years of Aztec rule had ended.

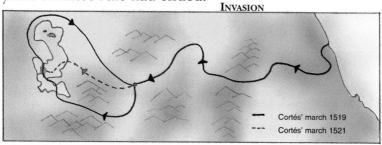

INVASION

— Cortés' march 1519
- - - Cortés' march 1521

(Left) *Cortés and his Spanish soldiers made two long marches through difficult territory to reach the Aztecs' great capital city, Tenochtitlan.*

Cortés first reached the city in 1519, but the Aztec defenders forced him to retreat. He attacked again in 1521, and captured it.

IN 1517 Hernando Cortés, future conqueror of Mexico, left Spain to seek his fortune. Like many Europeans, he believed the tales of a rich New World that Columbus told after his voyage of 1492. He was certain he would find gold in this New World, and did not care about Native American peoples or their way of life.

To Cortés and his soldiers **(left)**, Aztec lands were strange and hostile. They knew they were outnumbered by the Aztec people, so they were deliberately brutal, to inspire fear. But Aztec warriors had little hope of winning against Spanish swords and guns.

Mexico became a Spanish colony in 1535. The land was given to Spanish settlers; like Cortés, they hoped to exploit its riches. Aztecs and other native peoples were forced to work for the new Spanish rulers, like slaves. Within 100 years, almost 90 percent of the Aztecs had died, killed by hunger and by European diseases. Spanish priests and missionaries forced the Aztecs to abandon their religion and tried to convert them to Christian beliefs.

Cortés and Montezuma met for the first time in November 1519. Montezuma gave Cortés rich gifts of gold. Cortés was delighted – here was proof of America's wealth. But he mistook the meaning of Montezuma's gift; Montezuma was showing the Spaniards how important he was. Misunderstandings like this caused bitterness between the Aztecs and Cortés's men.

The citizens of Tenochtitlan hated the Spaniards for their arrogance, cruelty, and dishonesty.

Fighting broke out on July 10, 1520, after Spanish soldiers attacked Aztecs dancing outside the Great Temple.

The Spaniards were forced to flee. So many were killed that they called it "la Noche Triste," the Sad Night.

But Cortés survived. He made new plans, and besieged the city. Maybe 200,000 died before the Aztec leaders surrendered.

HELPFUL ALLIES

Cortés arrived in Mexico with about 500 soldiers. How could he hope to defeat the mighty Aztec army? He decided to befriend the Aztecs' chief enemies, the people of Tlaxcala.

The Tlaxcalans hated the Aztecs, because they took their soldiers as captives to be sacrificed. The Aztecs were also besieging Tlaxcala. The Tlaxcalans hoped Cortés would be able to stop this.

Cortés and the Tlaxcalans agreed to fight together against the Aztecs. When Cortés first met Montezuma, he was backed by a large army of Tlaxcalans, as well as his Spanish soldiers.

Q

How can the Spanish invasion of Mexico help us to discover more about Aztec life?
Go to pages 42-43

HOW DO WE KNOW?

WHEN SPANISH CONQUERORS first saw Tenochtitlan, they could hardly believe their eyes. "It was something I had never dreamed of before," wrote Cortés. Today, the city's houses, palaces, and even the lake have disappeared, buried under sprawling Mexico City. The Great Temple was pulled down by Spanish rulers, who used its stones to build a new cathedral.

Yet historians and archaeologists have discovered a great deal about the vanished Aztec people. On these pages is some of the evidence they have used.

(Left) Friar Bernardino de Sahagun spent years interviewing Aztec people to compile his mammoth book, A General History of the Things of New Spain. *It was completed by 1580. Although Sahagun used eyewitness reports, his findings are not always reliable. Many of his helpers had been terrorized by the Spanish invasion. They looked back to Aztec times as a glorious golden age.*

(Above) Bernal Diaz de Castillo was a soldier who traveled to Mexico with Cortés. He was also an historian, eager to record everything he saw. He wrote wonderfully detailed descriptions of Cortés's military campaigns, and of Tenochtitlan and its inhabitants, as he saw it before it was devastated during the Spaniards' siege of 1521. Diaz was very impressed by the Aztecs' wealth and good government. Later in life, in 1568, Diaz collected all his notes and reminiscences together, and wrote a famous book: The Conquest of New Spain. *Like Sahagun's, Diaz's work is one of our most important sources for studying Aztec life, even though it is written from a Spanish point of view.*

Codices, drawn by Aztec priests and scribes, provide especially important evidence of Aztec times. Unlike the Spanish historians, Aztec scribes understood the ceremonies and events they were describing. But even their work might be biased, depending on what the Tlatoani told them to record.

The 16th-century Codex Mendoza was made for Antonio Mendoza, Spanish governor of Mexico, to show the king of Spain what this newly conquered land was like. This page shows what Aztec warriors wore.

Although sixteenth-century Spaniards brought Aztec rule to an end, they did not destroy Aztec culture. Nahuatl, the Aztec language, is still spoken in Mexico. Mexican village women still wear embroidered blouses very like those worn by their Aztec ancestors, and still weave beautiful cloth using backstrap looms. And, even though most Mexicans now belong to the Roman Catholic church, elements of the Aztec religion remain. Paper flowers and skull-shaped candies still decorate tombs, as real flowers and real skulls once decorated Aztec temples.

In recent years, archaeologists have carried out major excavations in the heart of Mexico City (former Tenochtitlan) to investigate remains from the Aztec era. Other important finds, like the great carved Sun Stone (pictured on page

39), have been uncovered in the city by chance. Patient archaeological investigation has enabled us to understand more about Aztec crafts and building techniques, and to discover more about the Aztecs' daily life.

(Above) *There are few Aztec buildings still standing today. Most were* destroyed by the Spanish settlers, who wanted to remove all traces *of the Aztec past. This small temple at Santa Cecilia in northern Mexico* *City is the only Aztec temple to survive almost intact.*

The Aztecs' favorite foods – chilies, beans, avocado pears, sunflowers, and chocolate – are now eaten all around the world. And one of the Aztecs' own names for themselves, "Mexica," lives on in Mexico, the present-day name for the land where the Aztecs lived.

(Above) *Chacmool figures like this are found at temples throughout Middle America. They were probably carved to contain human hearts offered in sacrifices. They show that the Aztecs shared beliefs with peoples living nearby, and* with the great Toltec civilization of the past.

(Left) *Figures like this eagle knight, carved in stone and used to decorate the Great Temple in Tenochtitlan, let us see what Aztec warriors and worshipers might have looked like.*

(Right) *This statue of Xipe Totec, god of corn and productivity, shows what happened at one festival. Like the statue, priests or warriors wore the skin of a young man sacrificed to the gods. As the skin rotted, the corn would grow.*

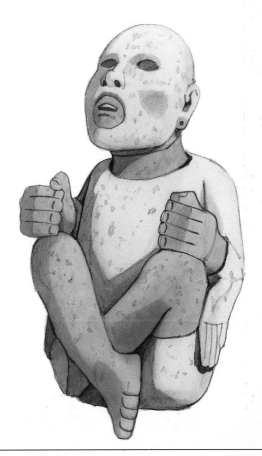

HAVE YOU SURVIVED?

Q1 Your father is getting dressed in a jaguar skin. Do you

A run away
B boast about it to your friends
C offer him some meat

Q2 Your parents are talking about Quetzalcoatl. Is this

A the start of an argument
B a place to visit
C an ancient priest-king, worshiped as a god

Q3 When you catch your first enemy do you

A win a medal
B cut him in pieces and take a bit home
C bury his body

Q4 What did the Aztecs call themselves?

A the Aztecs
B the Tlatoani
C the Mexica

Q5 Snake-Woman was

A a snake
B a woman
C a man

Q6 A neighbor refers to the Flowery Wars. Were these

A wars fought between the Aztecs and Tlaxcala
B mock battles using flowers instead of weapons
C when you wrecked a neighbor's chinampa

Q7 Your mother is making tortillas: will you use them to

A hit your brother with
B wear in your hair
C eat with stew

Q8 How many months in the farmers' year?

A 10
B 12
C 18

Q9 At school you are learning history. When studying the codices, do you read them

A like a book
B zigzag across the page
C upside down

Q10 Is your favorite drink

A nahuatl
B chocolatl
C titlitl

Q11 Was the New Fire ceremony held

A every 52 years
B every 25 years
C every 252 years

Q12 You are going to a calmecac. Will you be learning to be

A a priest
B a warrior
C a merchant

Q13 The Aztecs have no wheeled transportation. Was this because

A they hadn't invented the wheel
B they thought walking was good exercise
C the mountain roads were too steep

To find out if you have survived as an Aztec, check the answers on page 48.

THE AZTECS CLAIMED that they had lived in Mexico for centuries, and that Aztlan – a sacred cave in the north of the country – was their ancestral home. But historians are not sure exactly where Aztlan was, or where the Aztec people really came from. In fact, Aztec history before around 1345 remains rather mysterious, even today. But here are some dates that most historians agree about.

All dates A.D.

C.1111-C.1345 The Aztec people leave their original, unknown homeland, and wander in the desert in search of a better place to live.

C.1345 After fights with neighboring peoples, the Aztecs settle on a rocky island in the middle of Lake Texcoco, in the central valley of Mexico.

C.1345-1372 The Aztecs make alliances with powerful nearby states, though they aim to be independent one day. The city of Tenochtitlan expands. Chinampas are made and planted to grow food.

C. 1367 Start of reign of Acamapichtli, the first Aztec Tlatoani whose name is known for certain. For political reasons, he marries a princess from the rival Culhua people. She is descended from the ancient Toltec rulers of Mexico. He hopes this will win respect for the Aztecs. The next two Aztec rulers, Huitzilihuitl and Chimalpopoca, continue this policy of alliances with powerful peoples nearby.

1420s By now, Tenochtitlan is becoming crowded. There are problems with food and water supplies. Settlers leave the city to make homes on far shores of the lake. Traders settle on the nearby island of Tlatelolco.

1427-1440 Reign of Tlatoani Itzcoatl. He burned early Aztec codices because they showed that the first Aztecs had been rough and "uncivilized."

1428 Aztecs make Triple Alliance with other valley peoples – Texcoco and Tlacopan. Together they dominate Mexico. Other, smaller states are forced to pay tribute.

1440-1469 Reign of Montezuma I, the greatest Aztec Tlatoani. The Aztecs make more conquests.

1473 Traders' island of Tlatelolco captured by Aztecs; is a great market center for all Aztec lands.

1487 Temple redeveloped in center of Tenochtitlan. Aztec historians recorded that 20,000 captives were sacrificed there to the gods.

1490s New conquests, west of present-day Guatemala. Aztec power at its height.

1502 Montezuma II becomes Tlatoani. Ends Triple Alliance; Aztecs now the most powerful state in Mexico. Montezuma hears strange prophecy that the god Quetzalcoatl might return and destroy his power.

1519 Spanish adventurers, led by Hernando Cortés, arrive in Mexico. They plan to attack Tenochtitlan.

1520 Montezuma II invites Cortés to live in Tenochtitlan. Later, Montezuma is killed mysteriously, because the Aztec people distrust his political judgment. The new Tlatoani dies of smallpox, brought by the Spanish.

1521 After a nine-week siege, Spanish troops capture Tenochtitlan. They are helped by the Aztecs' enemies from the nearby state of Tlaxcala.

1535 Mexico becomes a colony of Spain.

TIMESPAN

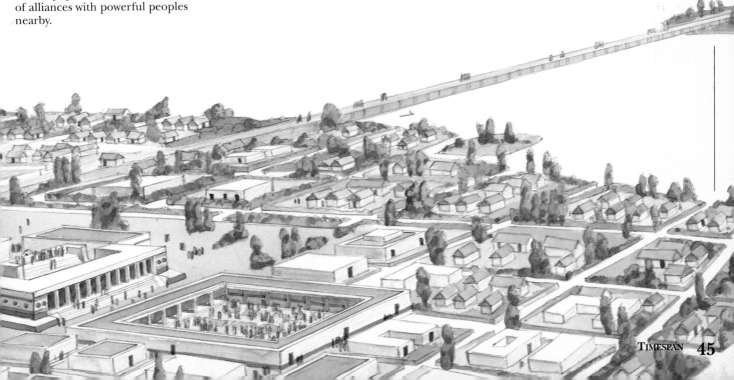

AQUEDUCT a channel built to carry water over long distances.

ASTRONOMY the science of observing the sun, moon, stars, and planets. The Aztecs believed the movements of the stars and planets foretold events on earth.

BARTER trading one sort of goods for others of equal value.

CALPULLI a social group, originally based on families. Traditionally, all calpulli members were believed to be descended from common ancestors. Later, calpulli membership depended on where you lived, rather than on who your ancestors were. Calpullis controlled land and important matters such as education, emergency food aid, and law and order.

CAUSEWAY a pathway raised above the level of surrounding ground or water.

CHINAMPA land reclaimed from the marshy shallows close to the shores of the great lakes in the central valley of Mexico.

CIHUACOATL the deputy leader of the Aztecs.

CODEX (plural CODICES) Aztec books, made of long strips of cactus or fig-leaf paper or parchment, folded accordion-style. Codex pages are filled with picture writing in brightly colored paints and inks. They contain history, astronomy, and legal and religious records.

COPAL strong-smelling incense, made from resin from trees, burned in Aztec temples to create a religious mood and to disguise the smell of blood.

FERMENT to produce alcohol through the action of yeast on sugar in a plant.

FLAYING removing the skin from the body of a person or an animal. Some Aztec religious ceremonies in honor of Xipe Totec involved flaying a sacrificial victim. As his skin decayed, the Aztecs believed new crops would grow.

GENEALOGY the record of a person's ancestors, showing whom they were descended from.

GODS the Aztecs believed that the world was created and controlled by divine (holy) power. They gave this power many different names, such as Huitzilopochtli (god of war), Tlaloc (god of rain), Xilonen (goddess of corn). Each god was honored by statues, temples, festivals, and sacrifices. But although they were worshiped separately, the Aztecs believed these gods were all different forms of the same holy power.

INCAS a powerful South American people, who, during the 13th and 16th centuries, lived in the region of present-day Bolivia and Peru.

IRRIGATE provide with water, so that crops can grow. The Aztecs dug channels to bring water from the mountains to fields in the valleys below.

LIMEWATER crushed limestone mixed with water.

LITTER a portable bed, used to carry the most important people in Aztec society.

MOSAIC a work of art made out of hundreds of tiny stone fragments carefully pieced together.

MUMMY BUNDLE an Aztec corpse, carefully wrapped in cloth and decorated with flowers and paper cutouts, ready for burial or burning.

OBSIDIAN a glassy rock, produced when volcanoes erupt. Used by the Aztecs for jewelry, weapons, and domestic and sacrificial knives.

PECTORAL jewelry, such as brooches, pendants, or necklaces, worn on the chest.

PEYOTE Mexican cactus containing a powerful mind-altering drug, used in Aztec medicine.

SACRIFICE an offering made to please or to "feed" the gods. The Aztecs believed that the gods needed to be given blood (the "water of life") to

keep the world in existence; if sacrifices stopped, the world would end.

SKULL RACK rows of skulls – sometimes real, sometimes carved in stone – arranged outside Aztec temples. They reminded Aztec worshipers that life and death were closely connected. Sacrificing some people to the gods meant that, for everyone else, life could continue.

TAMALES soft cakes made of corn flour, filled with savory meat or vegetable stew.

TERRACES earthworks designed to make farming possible on steep

mountain slopes. A series of "steps" is built. Each holds a strip of earth kept in place by a low wall to stop the earth from being washed away by heavy rain.

TLATOANI the Aztec ruler. He governed the Aztec lands with the help of army commanders, leading noblemen, and a deputy, known as Cihuacoatl. They were usually chosen from one powerful noble family, but sons did not always succeed their fathers. Sometimes one brother followed another as ruler. It depended on who was strongest, and who could win most support among other leading nobles.

TORTILLA a pancake made from corn flour mixed with water.

TRIBUTE goods sent to the Aztec rulers from peoples they had conquered. If tribute was not sent, the Aztecs attacked.

VICTIM someone killed as an offering to the gods. The Aztecs believed that this was an honorable and glorious way to die.

VIGIL staying awake for long hours – usually all night – as part of a religious ceremony.

Here are the quiz answers, with pages to turn to if you need an explanation.

Q

1(B) - pages 32-33
2(C) - pages 36, 40
3(B) - pages 32-33
4(C) - page 43
5(C) - page 6
6(A) - pages 32-33
7(C) - pages 20-21
8(C) - page 39
9(B) - page 38
10(B) - page 21
11(A) - page 28
12(A) - page 36
13(C) - page 26

Count up your correct answers and find out what your survival rating is.

12 - 13 Excellent! You will do well.
10 - 11 Good. You will be a worthy citizen.
6 - 9 Fair. You have a lot to learn.
5 - 0 Terrible! You would have problems living in Aztec times.